# Nutty and Buddy

## KAREN S. GAMMAGE

**NUTTY AND BUDDY**

Copyright © 2024   Karen S. Gammage

All rights reserved. No part of this book may be used or reproduced by any means, graphic, electronic, or mechanical, including photocopying, recording, taping or by any information storage  retrieval system without the written permission of the author except in the case of brief quotations embodied in critical articles and reviews.

Because of the dynamic nature of the Internet, any web addresses or links contained in this book may have changed since publication and may no longer be valid. The views expressed in this work are solely those of the author and do not necessarily reflect the views of the publisher, and the publisher hereby disclaims any responsibility for them.

Library of Congress Control Number:
      Paperback:         979-8-89306-087-4
      eBook:            979-8-89306-088-1

Printed in the United States of America

# NUTTY AND BUDDY

**KAREN S. GAMMAGE**

# Contents

Chapter 1  The Tree Nest Comes Down ................................................................. 7

Chapter 2  A New Life .............................................................................................. 21

Chapter 3  New Names ............................................................................................. 27

Chapter 4  More Room ............................................................................................. 35

Chapter 5  Back To Nature Or Where We Belong ................................................ 42

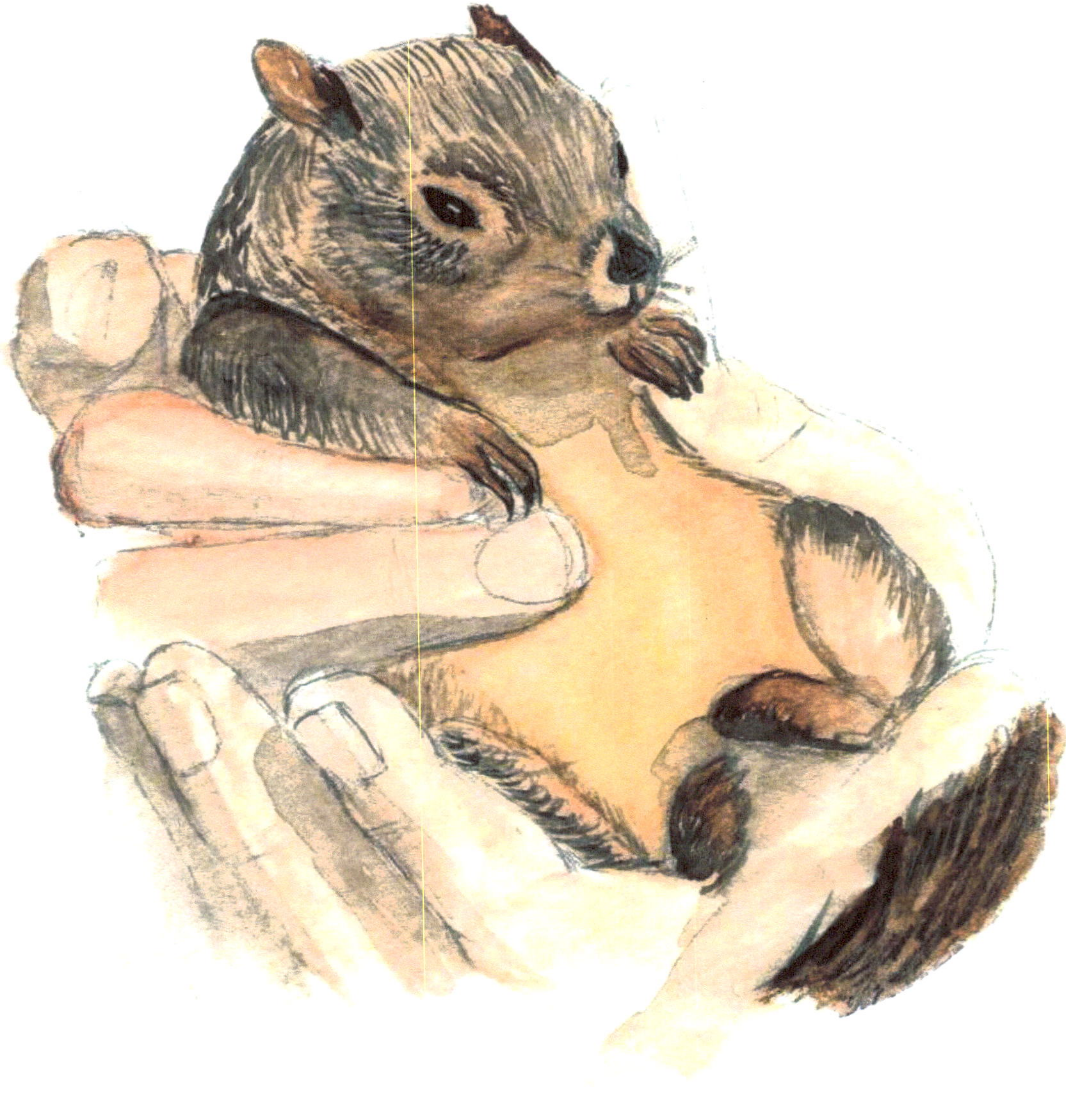

*Chapter 1*

# THE TREE NEST COMES DOWN

Two baby squirrels lived in a tall elm tree on a friendly brick laid street with lots of tall trees. Their mother made a soft nest out of straws and grass, in a hole, high on the trunk of the tree.

One day, while their mother was away from the nest gathering food, they felt an unusual shudder in the tree and loud noises.

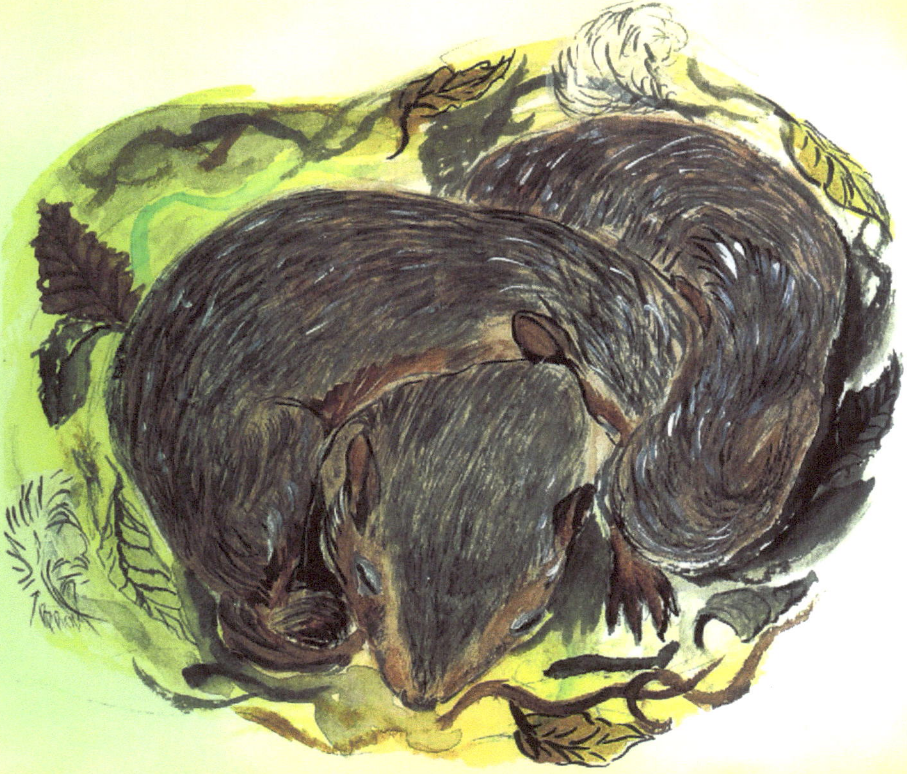

They were very frightened, as they had no idea what was happening, and they couldn't see yet. The baby squirrels were too young for their eyes to even be open.

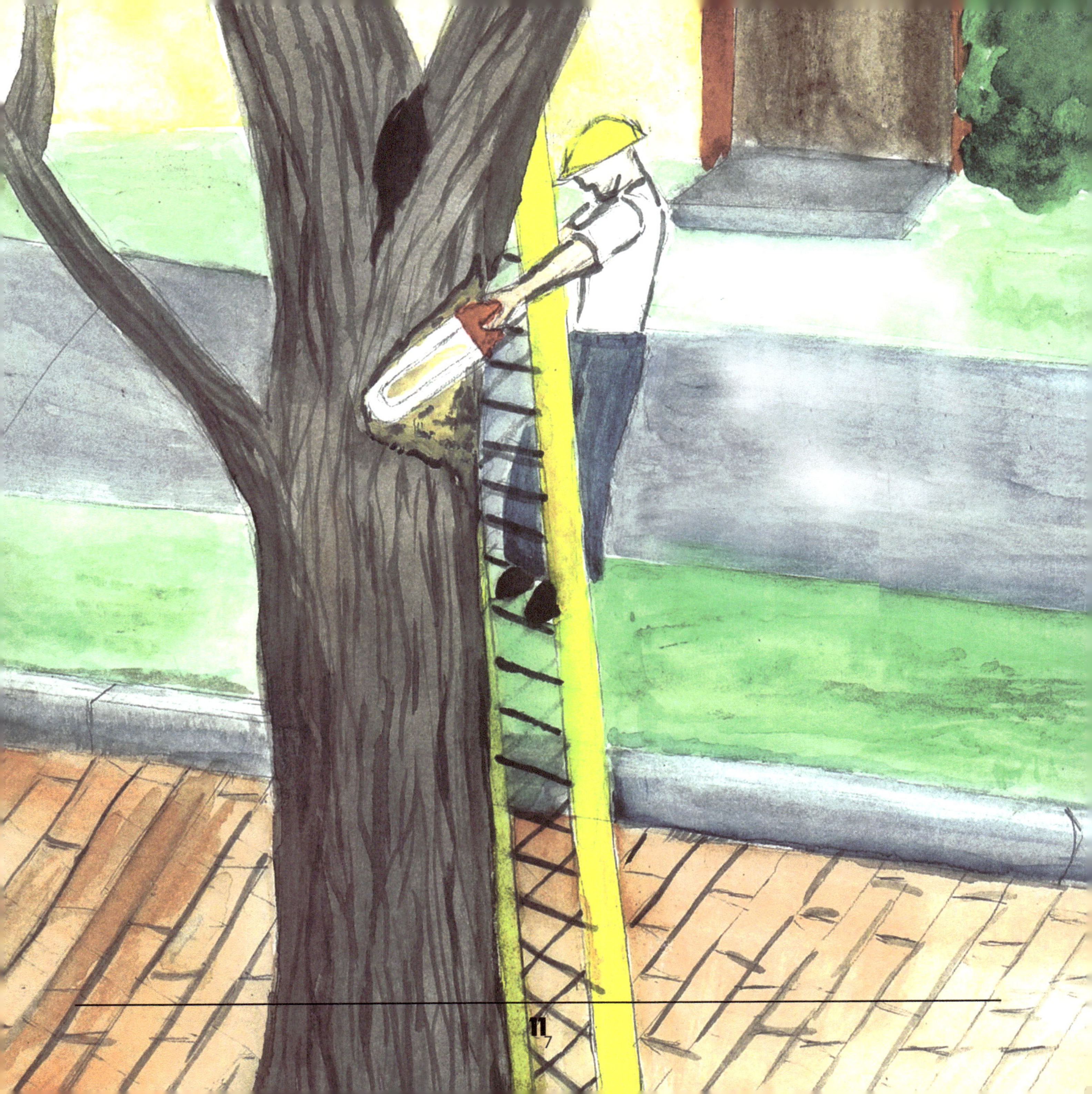

Squirrels are born with their eyes closed and they don't open until about six weeks of age. The tree shuddered again and men's voices were heard along with a loud buzz sound

13

This happened two or three times and then they suddenly felt themselves falling as they were flipped around inside the nest. The fall sharply stopped when the tree abruptly hit the ground with a hard thud. It bounced so hard that the baby squirrels were tossed out of the nest onto the ground rolling and rolling.

15

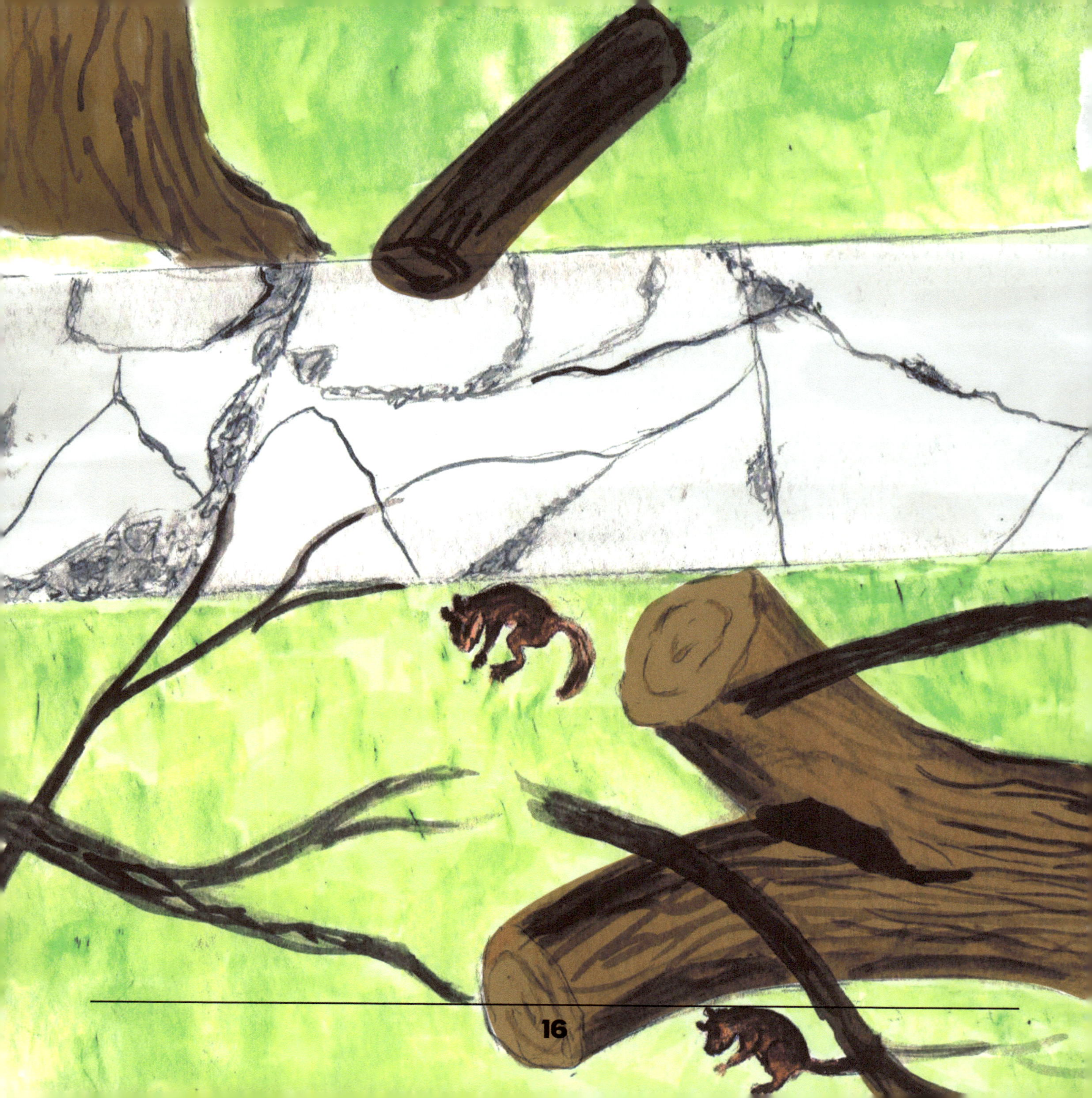

The largest of the baby squirrels was knocked out for a minute or two and was out of breath. He landed on the grass and was okay, but the smallest of the squirrels was not as lucky. He bounced out and hit his head hard on the sidewalk. He was not moving. The workmen jumped down to check on the squirrels right away. The boss told the other man to go and get the lady of the house.

The lady hurried out to see what was happening. When she saw the babies, she asked, "Are there any more?" The men said they didn't think so and set about lifting branches and checking to see if there were any others. When they were satisfied that there weren't more, they stated "We haven't found any more. We didn't know they were there until they hit the ground. The big one is moving but the little one isn't moving at all."

The lady stated, "I'm sorry that we cut down their nest but the tree had to come down. See the sidewalk. The tree roots have all of the sidewalks torn up and they are beginning to grow under the foundation of the house. We don't want the house wall to look like the sidewalk."

"Has anyone seen the mother squirrel?," someone asked. Everyone agreed that they had not seen the mother squirrel.

The lady said, "The babies will only survive if they are taken care of and fed. I'll run get a box to carry them and take them over to my sister-in-laws house. Gwyn is always taking care of injured animals and knows what to do."

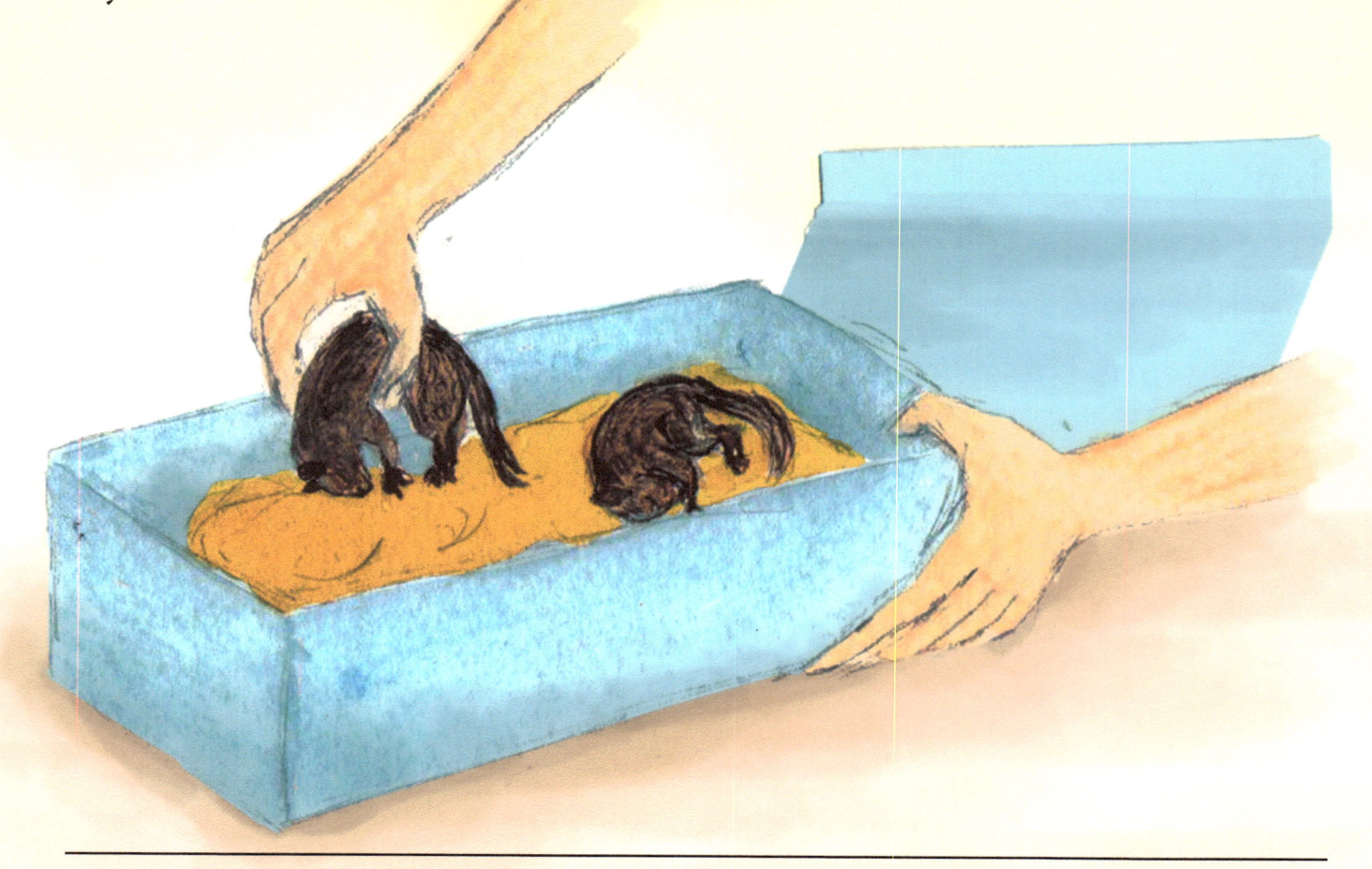

## Chapter 2

# A NEW LIFE

The baby squirrels felt a warm soft hand pick them up and place them in a shoebox on a soft towel to keep them comfortable. The smallest baby was still not responding, though he seemed to be breathing okay. The awake baby wobbled around and found the small sleeping baby squirrel in the box and snuggled close to him. The baby said to himself, "Momma, momma, where are you? Brother is hurt and I feel alone and scared, what do I do?" The box moved and then they were carried and placed in a car. They felt the car move. "What's happening?," thought the baby. This was a start of a very new life.

When they reached Gwyn's house, the lady said, "Here they are Gwyn. I hope you can help them. One is doing okay and the other one hasn't awakened yet since the fall. The workmen said that they were pretty sure that that baby hit his head on the sidewalk when he bounced out.

They look to be old enough that their eyes should be opening fairly soon."

Gwyn said cheerfully, "I think you're right. They do seem a good size. This little one I'm a bit worried about." She felt around on him to see if anything was broken and then she said, "I can feel a dent here, on his head.

I'm sure he hit the sidewalk. We'll just have to see how he does." Gwyn continued, as she tenderly cared for the baby squirrels, "I always enjoy taking care of baby squirrels. They are about the easiest wild animal to care for and return to the wild, if they are not over handled. I will need to go and get some goats milk.

I mix it with a special medicine water for sick children or babies. It works for most animals. In the mean time, I have a nice place for them."

"How often do babies that size need to be fed?," the lady asked.

Gwyn said, "About every two hours. Since this little one isn't awake, I'll have to feed him by giving him just a few drops at a time every 30 min. or so and give him time to swallow. I'll need to go very slowly with a dropper. The other squirrel will feed okay using a doll baby bottle

*Chapter 3*

# NEW NAMES

We'll need names for these little fellas won't we?" She thought for a minute and said, " I know. We'll call the little one Nutty and the big one Buddy."

Buddy took to being fed on the doll baby bottle quickly and was always ready to eat. Nutty slept for five whole days, with Gwyn dropping milk in his mouth, using a dropper, in small amounts, slowly and frequently. Nutty would swallow but he continued to sleep. On the fourth day Nutty made jerking motions and acted strange, but on the fifth day, Nutty awakened and acted like nothing had ever been wrong. He started eating and acting just like Buddy.

Both Nutty and Buddy opened their eyes the next week. Nutty opened his eyes about three days later than Buddy. As a matter of fact, Nutty did everything about three days after Buddy did as they matured and learned new things. They were delighted to see each other and loved each other. Nutty looked at Buddy and said, "Momma?"

"No, Silly, I'm your brother. You've been sleeping for five days, ever since we were tossed out of the nest," said Buddy. They were beginning to move around well on their own.

"Is that Momma?," inquired Nutty, while looking at Gwyn.

"I don't think so," said Buddy, "but she's very nice. We were brought here after the accident, by another lady. I don't think that was Momma either."

Gwyn's Border Collie, Jesse, was a true mother at heart.

Whenever Gwyn would bring home baby animals to care for, Jesse would help to raise the babies.

She would clean them like the mother, licking them tenderly, cleaning them and helping them to go to the bathroom. Mother animals do this for their babies until they can do it for themselves. Gwyn would feed them and set them on the floor then say, "Okay Jesse, do your thing. Jesse would tenderly tend to them as if she were their real mother. She would stand or lay by the cage and watch them, not letting other pets in the house close to the cage. Jesse helped to mother kittens, puppies, ferrets, and now squirrels. She just seemed to have an instinct to love babies no matter what they were.

Jesse said to the baby squirrels, "Don't worry babies, we'll take care of you. You'll be fine."

When Nutty and Buddy were a little older, Gwyn put a box in the corner of the cage, with some fur in it, so that they could make a nest. They were also starting to eat solid food. Nutty and Buddy began to hide food away in the nest, like squirrels are supposed to. Gwyn still had to feed them on the bottle, but now, only every four hours.

## Chapter 4

# MORE ROOM

They were beginning to need more room in which to move around. Squirrels need to climb and bounce to get strong muscles. One day, Gwyn let them out in the house and both Nutty and Buddy took off running and jumping great lengths. They bounced from the chair to the blinds and over to the couch chattering in squirrel talk all the time.

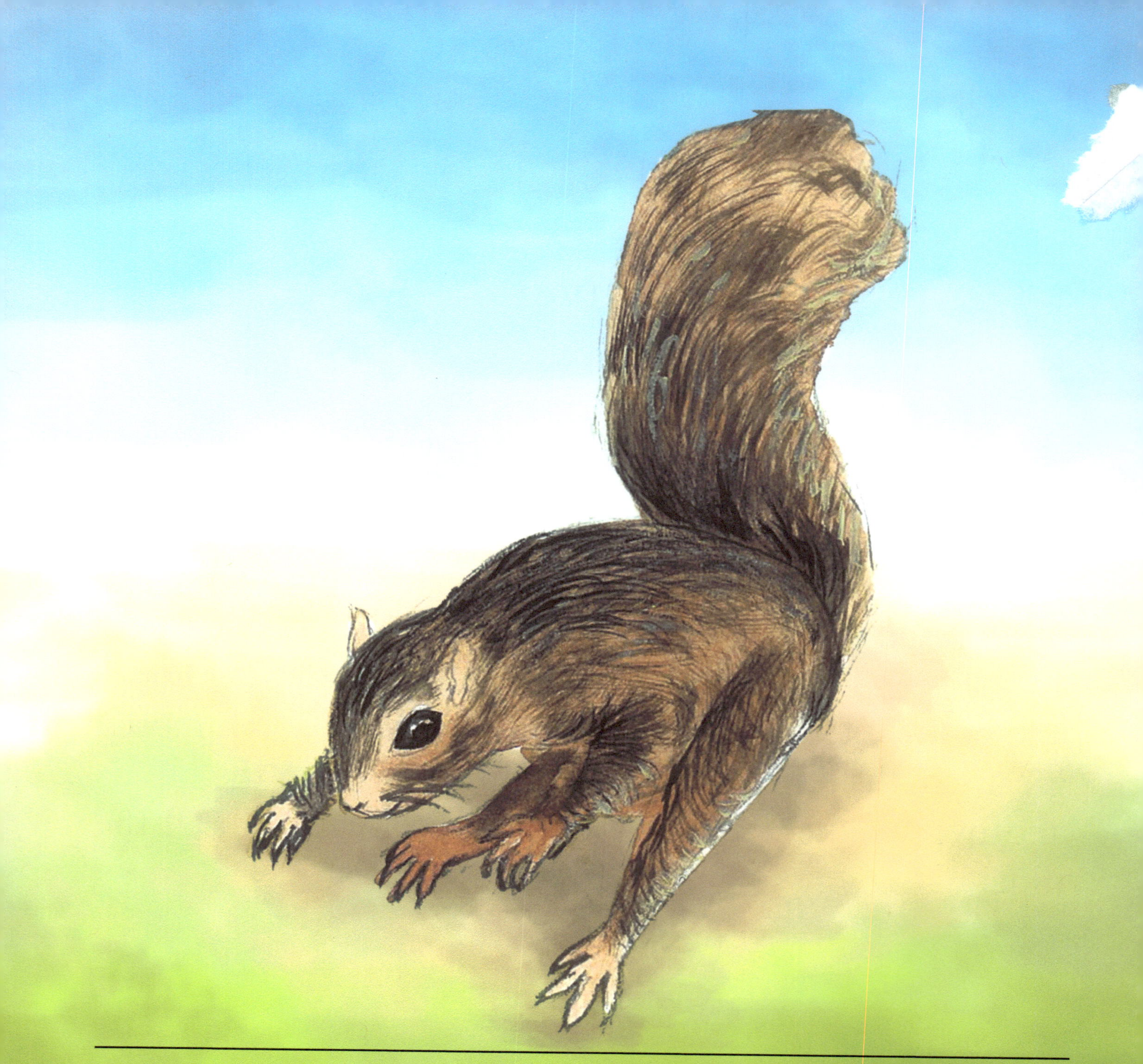

They hit the wall and back to the chair and onto the table. Buddy jumped onto Gwyn's shoulder and off again. Then Nutty jumped onto Gwyn's lap and over to the wall and back to the chair.

They bounced and climbed and climbed and bounced without stopping. It was great to be able to keep going and have a lot of room to try out their skills at keeping their balance and hanging on as well as bouncing. Gwyn said, " I think you need a larger cage and more limbs to climb on. I thought you might enjoy some space to stretch out in." Gwyn then built them a large cage outside the house that was about six foot by eight foot.

It was a bit like a dog run with smaller wire. She placed some large branches and some small branches in the cage along with their nest box. Gwyn kept a lot of peanuts, berries, fruit, sunflower seeds and vegetables in the cage. Nutty and Buddy were growing strong.

When winter came, it was decided that Nutty and Buddy were too small to take care of themselves in the wild. Nature teaches them to gather food and store it away for eating in the winter.

41

They had not had enough time to find a place to live. They had started learning to gather and store food in their nest box as Gwyn provided food in the cage. They would not have had enough time, to learn to locate food out in nature on their own, then gather and store sufficient food, as squirrels do, to have enough food to live on through the winter. They stayed in their large cage through the winter.

## Chapter 5

# BACK TO NATURE or WHERE WE BELONG

In the spring Nutty and Buddy were strong and healthy. They were able to take care of themselves. It was arranged that Nutty and Buddy would be taken to Gwyn's parent's house in the summer. Her parents lived in a small town and near a lake. There was enough food in the area for Nutty and Buddy to live on and to start to gather before winter again came. Her parents were excited to see some squirrels playing in their neighborhood. They had not had any squirrels there before. The big day came. Nutty and Buddy were placed back in the smaller cage with their nest box and taken to Gwyn's parent's house.

The cage was placed just outside the house. Some food was spread out on the ground so that Nutty and Buddy could see it. The cage door was opened and they were allowed to come out. Nutty and Buddy stood there for just a minute, looked at Gwyn, and then they took off running. Gwyn was a little sad to see them go and happy for them at the same time. She always wanted them to just be able to care for themselves and return to nature where they belonged. As a tear came to her eye, she waved at the squirrels and said,

45

"Goodbye. Be happy and take care of each other." The familiar cage with their nest box would stay there for a couple months until they found somewhere else to live and didn't need to come back to it. Gwyn's dad put food out for awhile so that there would be food for them until they didn't need it.

The first couple of times that Gwyn returned to check on Nutty and Buddy and she called to them, they came to her and ran up her leg and took food from her. After a year they no longer came to her when she called. They were seen in the neighborhood from time to time, happy and bouncing branch to branch. They were happily back in the wild.

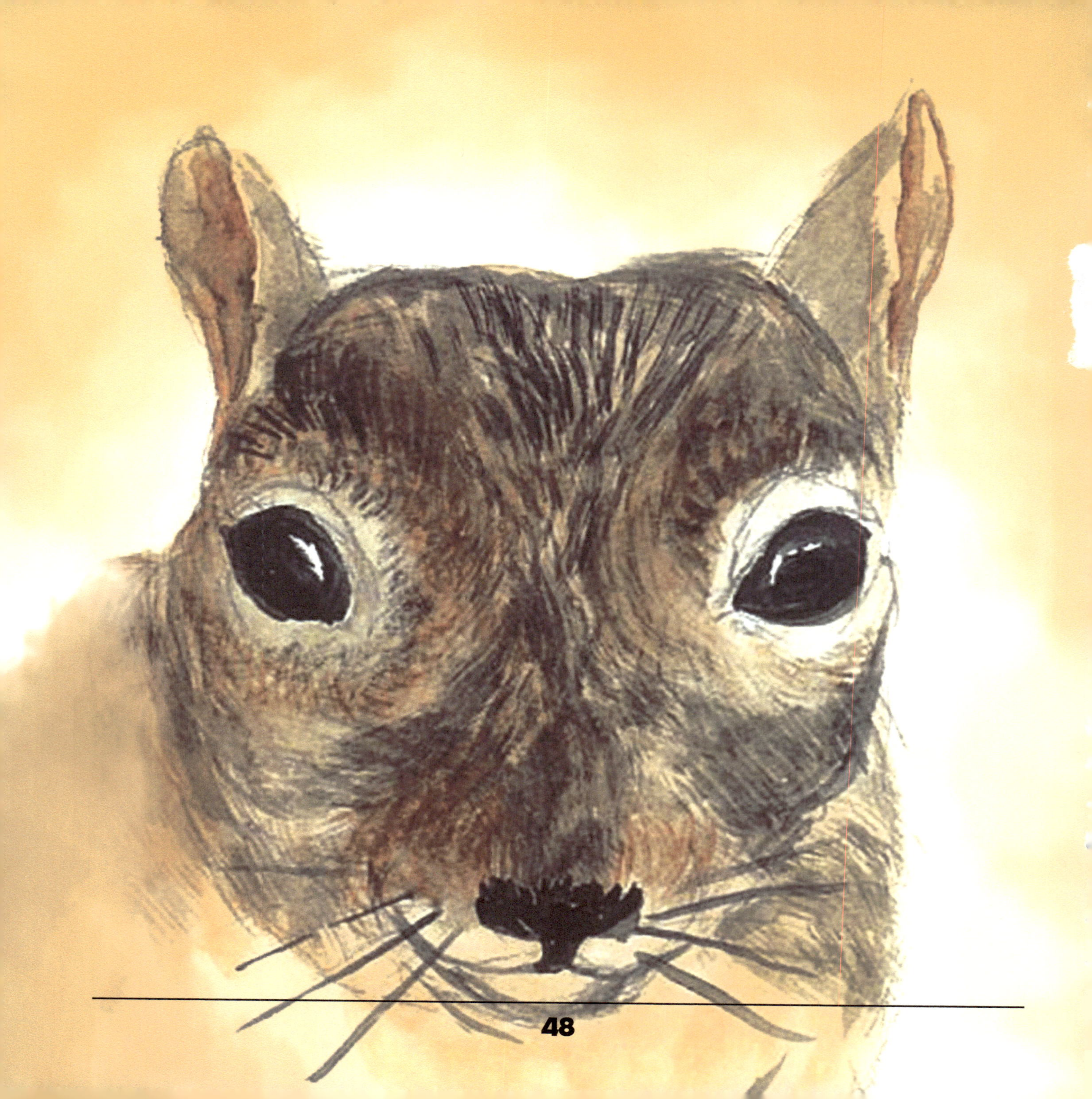

Milton Keynes UK
Ingram Content Group UK Ltd.
UKHW050716231124
451587UK00002B/13